CHILDREN
IN
ART

by Kate Sedgwick and
Rebecca Frischkorn

HOLT, RINEHART AND WINSTON
New York

To Tod and Carl

Copyright © 1978 by Kate Sedgwick & Rebecca Frischkorn

Printed in the United States of America
Designed by Joseph Bourke Del Valle

10 9 8 7 6 5 4 3 2 1

Library of Congress Cataloging in Publication Data

Sedgwick, Kate.
  Children in art.

  SUMMARY: A collection of stories, most of them based on true facts, about famous paintings and pieces of sculpture that depict children.
  1. Children in art—Juvenile literature. 2. Art appreciation—Juvenile literature. [1. Children in art. 2. Art appreciation] I. Frischkorn, Rebecca, joint author. II. Title. N7642.S4   757'.5
77-10883
ISBN 0-03-020896-3

Thanks are due to the children who visited the Huntington Galleries and Sunrise. You inspired us; we hope this inspires you.
Also, to our friend and editor, Miriam Chaikin, we thank you for never losing hope in our venture.

INTRODUCTION

The idea for this book came about when, working in separate museums, we made the same observations about how children reacted to works of art. We found that they were either afraid to approach a painting or piece of sculpture—as if such were not for the likes of them—or that, when they were led around the museum and fed facts about paintings, they grew bored.

Looking for ways to overcome this obstacle, we began to tell stories about the works of art. Instantly, the tours were enlivened. The children were interested and became enthusiastic. Often they would ask, when a tour was over, "Tell me again the story about the little boy with the blue bird in his hand."

The stories we told seemed to make a difference. Set in the context of a story, a painting or piece of sculpture seemed less formidable, more available.

Children in Art uses this technique to interest children in art history. This book is a collection of stories about famous paintings and pieces of sculpture, each a depiction of children. Most of the stories are based on true happenings. We have built the text around facts concerning the painting, its subject, or the life of the artist. Four accounts are pure fiction: "The Mason Children," "Don Manuel Osorio de Zuñiga," "The Watermelon Boys," and "A Dancer at the Age of Fourteen." For these works no facts could be found, so we drew fictional accounts around the subjects of the paintings.

In writing the book, we kept to a minimum the dates and other dry facts that often turn children away from art. Rather, we tried to point up the little-known facts that make art history memorable. Artists for centuries have cared about children; perhaps through the stories in this book, children can learn to care about the artists.

A note to children: **Don't** worry if you can't remember the name of a painting or the artist. **Just** enjoy what you see!

CONTENTS

CLEOBUS AND BITON 580 B. C.

POLYMEDES (pah-li-MEE-deez)

Delphi Museum, Delphi, Greece

Once upon a time in the faraway land of Argos in Greece there were two brothers, Cleobus and Biton. Their father was dead and they lived with their mother, whom they loved very much.

One day the people of Argos were preparing to celebrate the festival of Hera, who was queen of the gods. So, too, were Cleobus and Biton and their mother getting ready to celebrate. However, when it came time to go, the ox was missing. There was no way for them to get to the temple. The mother was very upset. She had been looking forward to going to the festival. Now she would have to miss it. Cleobus and Biton did not like to see their mother sad.

They hitched themselves to the cart and, with their mother seated inside, dragged the cart all the way to the temple of the goddess high in the mountains.

When they reached the temple and people saw what they had done, men praised the boys, and women told the mother how lucky she was to have such good, loving sons. The mother was happy. She went to the temple of Hera and asked the goddess to give her sons the greatest happiness man can have.

That night the two boys died in their sleep. At first their mother was hurt and angry with the goddess. She had prayed for her sons' happiness. Instead, the goddess had killed them. The goddess appeared to the mother and said, "I have bestowed upon your sons the greatest honor in the world; they will be admired forever and never be forgotten. Already the people are carving statues of the two boys to honor them."

The goddess fulfilled her promise. Today, 2,500 years later, Cleobus and Biton are still admired by all who see the statues that the people of Argos made in honor of the two good boys.

6

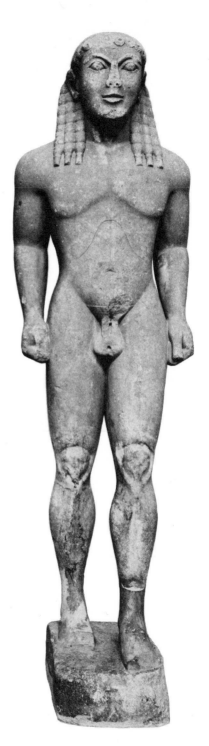

DAVID 1408–09

DONATELLO (dah-nuh-TELL-oh)

National Museum, Florence, Italy

Long ago in the city of Bethlehem lived a young shepherd named David. His wish was to visit the battlefield where King Saul was leading the Israelites against the Philistines. At last, David convinced his father to send him bearing gifts of corn, bread, and cheeses to the army.

At the battlefield, the giant Goliath had challenged any of Saul's soldiers to combat. Saul could not win the war so long as Goliath was alive, yet no Israelite came forward to fight him. They were afraid. The eight-foot-tall giant had never been defeated. David offered to kill the giant.

King Saul gave David a fine suit of armor, a helmet, and a bronze sword. But David turned them aside. The armor was too heavy, and he was not trained for war. As a shepherd he often had to shoot rocks at wild bears or lions that threatened his sheep.

Carrying his sling and shepherd's staff, David set out to meet the giant. But first he stopped by a stream and chose two or three perfect stones as ammunition.

Goliath was furious to see that a little shepherd boy had come to fight him. David taunted the giant, running near and shouting insults at Goliath. He did this again and again. When Goliath, hot and frustrated, raised his helmet to wipe the sweat from his forehead, David saw his chance. He swung his sling and sent a stone straight to the giant's head. As Goliath fell, David seized his sword, and cut off his head.

David became the hero of the Israelites. King Saul honored David and gave him his daughter as a wife. After Saul died, David became king and ruled Israel wisely and well for forty years, until he died.

MADONNA AND CHANCELLOR ROLIN around 1434

JAN VAN EYCK (van IKE)

Louvre, Paris, France

The three figures in this painting are the baby Jesus, his mother Mary, called the Madonna, and Nicolas Rolin, chancellor to the Flemish duke Philip the Good. They are sitting in a richly decorated upstairs room in a Romanesque palace. In this painting, which Van Eyck made for the duke, the chancellor is fifty-eight years old.

Notice how the figures of the two grown-ups balance each other. Above Mary's head an angel holds a richly carved crown. Balancing this, above the chancellor's head is a series of carvings showing scenes from the first book of the Bible.

But the most important element is the baby, Jesus. He is naked and his body shines brightly. The chancellor and the Madonna fade into their dark, plain backgrounds. The baby's background is bright and very intricate. The figure of Jesus stands out. Van Eyck painted an orb in the hand of Jesus to show that he is the creator of the World. The landscape behind him is his creation.

See how the painter has carefully shown every tiny detail. Look at how perfectly he painted the hem on Mary's robe and the chancellor's fur collar. Van Eyck is thought to have been the inventor of oil painting. Painters before him had to "draw" with tempera paints, laying one brushstroke next to another. With oil painting, Van Eyck could apply layers of paint to get rich color and a feeling of light and dark. Because of this Van Eyck is considered the master of Flemish painting.

12

CHILDREN'S GAMES 1560

PIETER BRUEGHEL THE ELDER (BROI-guhl)

Vienna Kunsthistorisches Museum, Vienna, Austria

The children in this picture lived in Holland over four hundred years ago. Yet many of the games they were playing are still played today. Can you find all the different games?

rolling hoops?   blowing balloons?
playing leapfrog?   playing marbles?
making mudpies?   riding a stick horse?
playing a drum?   playing piggyback?
playing dress-up?   playing jacks?
doing somersaults?   playing blindman's buff?
guessing which hand?   playing tag?   climbing trees?
having cockfights?   standing on their heads?
playing ball?   spinning tops?   walking on stilts?
swinging on a rail?   making a train?
swimming?   playing king of the mountain?   rolling a barrel?
playing hide and go seek?   climbing a fence?
wrestling?   parading?
juggling?
What else do you see?

There is only one grown-up in the whole painting. Can you find her? She is leaning out of the side window of the house, throwing water on two boys who are fighting!

LAS MENINAS
(The Maids of Honor) 1656

DIEGO RODRÍGUEZ DE SILVA Y VELÁZQUEZ (vuh-LAS-kes)

The Prado, Madrid, Spain

Princess Margarita was bored. She was tired of playing with her ladies-in-waiting and with the two dwarfs, Nicolasita Pertusato and Maria Barbola. She wanted to see her parents, the king and queen.

"But, Princess," said a lady-in-waiting who was watching the children play, "you can't see your parents now."

"Why not?" asked the angry little princess.

"They are posing for their portrait by the great artist, the master Velázquez. We must not disturb them!"

Without a word, the princess darted out of the nursery, her dog behind her. She ran toward the portrait gallery, where she saw her parents, King Philip IV and Queen Mariana, posing for Velázquez, the great artist. She stood watching.

The servants chased after her.

"Please come back with us to the nursery, Princess Margarita," begged a lady-in-waiting. The two dwarfs tried to make her laugh, to get her back to the nursery. The older lady-in-waiting and a manservant whispered among themselves, not knowing what to do. But the princess would not move.

The king and queen caught sight of their pretty little daughter in the mirror. Trying not to move their heads, so as not to disturb the painter, they looked ahead and smiled at each other in the mirror. They were happy to see her too.

THE MASON CHILDREN 1670

ARTIST UNKNOWN

Anonymous Collection

"Alice, Alice, I don't look like that!" squealed Hannah.

"No," said Alice, "we all look so stiff."

Jeptha reminded his sisters what their father had told them about the painter. He is called a limner, a person who travels around painting family portraits. Mr. Mason, the children's father, had not had a portrait painted since the family left England.

"Our dresses sent from England look so lovely," Alice said. "But I still don't understand why Hannah held the rose and I held the fan and beads, and why you, Jeptha, were painted with Father's cane."

"Don't you remember? Those objects are signs. A rose and a fan with beads are the signs for a girl. The cane is a sign for a boy. Since boys often wear long dresses until they are two or three years old, what we hold in our hands shows whether we are boys or girls."

Hannah pointed to the dates on the painting. "We'll always know how old we were when we were painted," she said. "The limner put our ages above each of us. I am four, Alice is six, and Jeptha is eight, and the year we were painted is above Jeptha. That is 1670."

MASTER CREWE AS HENRY VIII 1776

SIR JOSHUA REYNOLDS

Collection of Lord O'Neill, Antrim, N. Ireland

"Look carefully at this portrait of King Henry VIII," said Sir Joshua Reynolds, handing Master Crewe some clothes.

"Do you want me to dress up in these?" asked Master Crewe.

"Yes. Dressed in his costume, you will look exactly like the king. Then I will paint your portrait, as Hans Holbein painted King Henry's."

"Where do I begin?" said Master Crewe excitedly.

"Put on the short white stockings King Henry always wore," Sir Joshua began. "Then the shoes with the large brass buckles."

"You'll have to help me with this," Master Crewe said, handing Sir Joshua the heavy dress. Sir Joshua slipped the dress over Master Crewe's head. The boy laughed. "It's the heaviest dress I've ever worn."

"All the stones and golden thread make it heavy," said Sir Joshua. Master Crewe then tied the knife around his waist with the golden cord. And over his dress he put the velvet cape, just like the one King Henry was wearing. It was scarlet, the color for royalty.

"Don't forget your favorite hat with the rabbits' fur on it," said Sir Joshua.

Master Crewe looked himself over, then looked at the portrait of King Henry. "I look just like the king, don't I?" he exclaimed.

18

"There's one difference," Sir Joshua said. "King Henry didn't have puppies at his feet."

"Oh, but I want my puppies painted with me," Master Crewe said. And Sir Joshua obliged Master Crewe and left the puppies there.

Sir Joshua Reynolds based this painting on the portrait of King Henry VIII by Hans Holbein. This story describes how the painter and his young model might have planned the painting together.

PORTRAIT OF TWO CHILDREN
About 1750

JOSEPH BADGER

Abby Aldrich Rockefeller Folk Art Collection, Williamsburg, Virginia

Usually artists sign their paintings. However, in the 1700's, folk artists—artists with no formal training—rarely did so. If a painting is unsigned, it is necessary to become something of a detective to find out who the painter was.

Joseph Badger was an artist painting at that time. This painting, called *Portrait of Two Children,* is not signed. Even so, Mr. Badger is thought to be the artist. And the children are believed to be Stephen and Relief Brown. Why? Because Mr. Badger made a portrait of Captain and Mrs. Brown at around the same time. And these children look exactly like that couple.

Another clue lies in the costumes that the children wear. And in the squirrel on a chain, held by Stephen, and the coral and silver bells, held by Relief. Mr. Badger used those very articles and costumes in other portraits he painted.

DON MANUEL OSORIO de ZUÑIGA 1788

FRANCISCO JOSÉ DE GOYA Y LUCIENTES (GOI-ah)

Metropolitan Museum of Art, New York, New York

I wish I didn't have to stand here, posing for this picture.

I don't like this stiff red suit. The lace scratches me and I feel silly. I don't like being so fancy. And I really am tired.

And I'm so scared for my pet bird. The painter promised me the cats won't hurt her, but their eyes are beady and mean, and they inch closer each minute. They're right next to her now, ready to pounce. I really don't like this.

The painter, Señor Goya, *is* nice, though. He's a friend of Father's. He's supposed to be very famous. He loves children, I think. They say he has lots of children of his own. I know by the way he talks he likes me too. He says kind things and funny things to make me smile.

All the same, I wish I didn't have to stand here any longer.

THE PEACEABLE KINGDOM
1830—40

EDWARD HICKS

Worcester Art Museum, Worcester, Massachusetts

Isaiah 11:6: The wolf also shall dwell with the lamb, and the leopard shall lie down with the kid; and the calf and the young lion and the fatling together; and a little child shall lead them.

Edward Hicks was a Quaker, and he trusted the words of the Bible as the truth. To him these words described perfectly the peace and harmony of nature. Ordinarily a wolf would try to eat a lamb and a tiger would growl fiercely if anyone tried to hold him down. But these animals are quiet and good. It is a scene of perfect peace. The little child who will lead them is Christ and the perfect peace is the Kingdom of Heaven.

Mr. Hicks added other figures to the painting to tell us even more about his vision of peace. The fat man in the left wearing a three-cornered hat is William Penn. And the sheet of paper he is holding is his peace treaty with the Indians. This scene tells that *Penn*sylvania, which means "Penn's Woods," has been founded. Its capital will be Philadelphia, which means "The City of Brotherly Love."

Edward Hicks was not a trained artist, and he probably had never seen a lion or a leopard, but he wanted to paint a picture of his idea of heaven. He painted the "peaceable kingdom" more than one hundred different ways. Each is a little different, but each has the same message: *peace*.

THE FIFER 1866

EDOUARD MANET (ma-NAY)

The Louvre, Paris, France

"Guess what!" Cam boasted proudly to his brother, Peter. "I'm going to have my portrait painted in my fifer's uniform."

"Surely you're joking!" exclaimed Peter.

"I'm not," Cam said. "Mr. Manet wants to paint a fife player from the Imperial Guard and Commander Lejosne has chosen *me* over everyone else."

"Why you?" Peter asked.

"Actually, I think it's only my fifer's uniform Mr. Manet wants to paint, but at least I am the one chosen for it," Cam said. "Commander Lejosne told me to have my red breeches clean so the blue stripes down the side will show. I must polish the brass buttons on my coat, and wipe it free of every speck of dust. My military hat with the gold tassel must be just so on my head, and I can't move because my gold fife case will slide down my white silk sash."

"It sounds like a lot of trouble to me," said Peter.

"Oh, I'm so excited, I'll go to any trouble." Cam laughed. "Mr. Manet is a famous painter. He likes everything in perfect place when he's painting."

Peter was allowed to watch his brother's portrait being painted by Mr. Manet. But he was shocked and surprised when he saw the finished painting several years later at a gallery in Paris called Place de l'Alma. The uniform was his brother's, but the boy inside it did not have his brother's face. Mr. Manet had used his stepson, Léon Koella, to pose for the face of "The Fifer."

HARMONY IN GRAY AND GREEN:
Portrait of Miss Cicely Alexander 1872-73

JAMES ABBOTT McNEILL WHISTLER

Tate Gallery, London, England

August 3, 1924

Dear Eleanor,

Thank you so much for writing to me. I am glad you are studying Mr. Whistler in your art class and glad you like the painting he did of me.

In the picture I am nine years old. No, I was not very sad when it was painted. Rather, I was very tired of standing still and posing. Mr. Whistler made me pose over seventy days for this painting. I had to stand very still for hours at a time, and not even move my head. He was very particular and even picked out my costume and told Mummy where to have it laundered.

. . . I used to get very tired and cross, and often finished the day in tears. . . . Although he was rather inhuman about letting me stand on for hours and hours, he was most kind in other ways. . . . I was too young to appreciate Mr. Whistler himself, though afterwards we were very close friends. . . .

You asked why Mr. Whistler did not sign his name to the painting. . . . if he was so proud of it. He did! Look very carefully at the wall in the left side of the picture and you will see a butterfly. This is how Mr. Whistler signed his name and he became famous for it.

I'm glad you like this painting, Eleanor, because I do too. I am an old lady now and have been painted many times in my life, but this is my very favorite painting of me.

Please write me again if you have any more questions. I would love to hear from you.

Fondly,
Cicely Alexander Spring-Rice

29

THE WATERMELON BOYS 1876

WINSLOW HOMER

Cooper Hewitt Museum, New York, New York

Sliding under barbed wire fences
Sneaking into a watermelon patch
Trying not to be caught.
Whispering softly
Punching each melon
Picking the pinkest, juiciest melon that ever was.
Spitting black seeds
Slurping, drooling,
Delighting in our find.

MADAME CHARPENTIER AND HER CHILDREN 1878

PIERRE-AUGUSTE RENOIR (ren-WAHR)

Metropolitan Museum of Art, New York, New York

"Mummy, Mummy, Mr. Renoir is in the salon and is ready to paint us. Please, can my dog Bozo be painted too?" Georgette pleaded.

"You must ask Mr. Renoir," replied Madame Charpentier. "He needs quiet when he is painting portraits."

"Mr. Renoir, if Bozo is very still, can I sit upon his back?" Georgette asked.

Renoir laughed. "But what if Marguerite wants to sit on Bozo too? You can't both sit there!" he said.

"Oh, she won't. She wants to sit next to Mummy. I think she's afraid of your long beard."

"Well, well." He chuckled. "Now I know why your mother wrote only last week asking me to have it trimmed."

Marguerite blushed. "Mr. Renoir, are you our uncle?" she asked.

"No, a devoted friend of your father's," replied Renoir. "I met him when I was trying to sell my paintings on the sidewalk. I needed money to pay my rent. Georges, your father, bought a scene of Paris. He liked my work and invited me to visit him and to be introduced to other artists and poets.

"Now he has asked me to paint you, your sister, and your lovely mother. This will help me because Monsieur Charpentier will show this painting to his friends. I hope they will like it and ask me to paint their families."

Mr. Renoir's hope came true. After painting "Madame Charpentier and Her Children," he received many commissions to paint women and children. These paintings helped him to become famous as a formal portrait painter.

33

34

WOMAN AND CHILD DRIVING 1879

MARY CASSATT (kuh-SAT)

Philadelphia Museum of Art, Philadelphia, Pennsylvania

Mary Cassatt was an American painter. At a young age, she and her family moved to Paris from Philadelphia. Soon after their move, Alexander, Mary's brother, gave his parents money to buy a pony and cart. The pony was named Bichette. Everyone loved Bichette, especially Mary. She was a good horsewoman and rode every day, until she was hurt in a riding accident and had to give it up.

In this painting, Mary shows her sister, Lydia, driving the cart. The little girl beside Lydia is Odile Fevre, Degas's niece. The groom for the horse sits stiffly behind Lydia, ready to help if he is needed. They are driving in the Bois de Boulogne, a huge forest park in Paris.

A DANCER AT THE AGE
OF FOURTEEN 1880

EDGAR DEGAS (duh-GAH)

Metropolitan Museum of Art, New York, New York

I am a dancer in the ballet. Every day since I was five years old
I've practiced for hours and hours. It's always the same:

> First position, plié low,
> And my arms must be just so;
> Demi-plié, arabesque,
> Repeat again, no time to rest.

Madame, my teacher is kind, but she's strict. If I make just the
smallest mistake, I must begin again and do it over and over.
That's the only way for a dancer to learn. A dancer must be
perfect.

Sometimes I'm so sore and tired that I want to cry. Sometimes I wonder if it's worth all the work. But when the perform-
ance comes, and I'm dressed in my beautiful costume, and I'm
dancing my best, and I hear the audience clapping, *then* I'm
glad I'm a dancer. I love the ballet. I love to dance.

CARNATION, LILY, LILY, ROSE 1886

JOHN SINGER SARGENT

Tate Gallery, London, England

Elizabeth and Jessica ran out into the garden to help with the final decorations. It was Elizabeth's first Midsummer's Eve party. Midsummer's Eve—the longest day of the summer, the day all the fairies leave their hiding places to come out and dance, the most magical day of the year.

"If it's almost time, we can light the Japanese lanterns," said Jess. "Papa taught me how and I'll show you, but we'd better be careful."

"Won't they catch fire?" asked Elizabeth.

"Oh, no," said Jessica, "not if we do it just the right way. You push up from the bottom and the candle inside comes through the hole at the top. That way, it doesn't touch the paper on the sides." She used the taper to light her candle, then let the bottom down carefully. "There, it's lit," she said. The candle burned strong as the lantern swayed softly in the summer breeze.

"Oh, they're all so beautiful." Elizabeth sighed. "I've never seen anything more beautiful, even the Christmas tree with all its candles."

"Girls, are you almost finished?" their father called from the porch, where he was busy lighting a string of lanterns.

"Almost, Papa," called Jess, and the two girls set to work lighting the rest of the Japanese lanterns in the garden.

When they lit the last lantern, the girls stood back to admire their work. The lanterns flickered and glowed throughout the garden. It seemed very magical to Elizabeth, and she began to sing the popular summertime song:

"Fairies dancing while the sunset glows,
Carnation, Lily, Lily, Rose."

BABY'S PARTY 1903

HENRI ROUSSEAU (rew-SOH)

Winterthur Museum, Winterthur, Switzerland

Q.–What do you call the puppet that the baby is holding?
A.–A marionette!
Q.–Can you find where the artist signed his name?
A.–Yes! Down in the corner, under the marionette's feet.
Q.–What is the artist's name?
A.–Henri Rousseau!
Q.–Is the baby a boy or a girl?
A.–We don't know!
Q.–Is the baby happy or sad? Smiling or mad?
A.–What do you think?
Q.–Does this look like a real baby?
A.–It doesn't to me! To me it looks like a giant baby or a tiny grown-up. What do you think?

There is no "right" answer. You can answer however you like. A riddle is a question with a funny answer, one you didn't expect. Sometimes looking at art can be like answering riddles. There is a great deal of confusion about the life of Henri Rousseau. Not much is known about him. It is known that he was a toll collector in a customs house and that he never received formal art instruction. But people disagree on most other facts. His lawyer, Maître Guilhermet, representing him in court, could only say, "My client, Mr. Rousseau, has been a complete riddle to me!" You can approach Mr. Rousseau as a riddle. Use your imagination. And, most important, have fun! Rousseau did!

THE SPIELERS 1905

GEORGE LUKS (lewks)

Addison Gallery of American Art

Phillips Academy, Andover, Massachusetts

A man in New York was passing a group of children playing on the sidewalk. He heard the children mention the name of George Luks. Luks was his friend, so he stopped to listen.

"George Luks ain't a goin' to paint you!"

"Why ain't he a goin' to paint me? My mama dressed me all nice."

"Huh, that's why—he ain't a goin' to paint no kids what's clean."

Later the man met the artist and he asked why the children had said this. Mr. Luks replied he didn't like children to sit stiffly and pose. He liked to paint children naturally—as they play.

In "The Spielers," children in everyday clothes are dancing to the music of an organ grinder and are having a wonderful time. They are not dressed in fancy party dresses.

These girls and their friends are the children whom George Luks liked to paint. He painted many children who were playing on the sidewalks in his neighborhood in New York City.

ROCKING CHAIR #3 1950

HENRY MOORE

Collection of Henry Moore, Much Hadham, Hertfordshire, England

Grown-ups use a rocking chair as children use a rocking horse. They ride it to distant places and dream.

Here, a mother and child ride together. If they were in England, the mother would sing:

> Ride a cockhorse to Banbury Cross,
> To see a fine lady upon a white horse.
> With rings on her fingers and bells on her toes,
> She shall have music wherever she goes.

If they were in the United States, the mother might sing:

> Trot-trot to Boston,
> Trot-trot to Lynn,
> Trot-trot to Salem,
> And then trot home again.

Henry Moore made this sculpture and two others like it as toys for his four-year-old daughter, Mary. They really rock! When he was making them he discovered he could make them rock faster or slower by changing the curvature of the base and the weights of the figures. Imagine all three rocking together. What wonderful toys!

FARAWAY 1952

ANDREW WYETH (WY-uth)

Private Collection

Jamie was all bundled up in his warm winter clothes sitting on the hillside beyond his house. But his mind was far, far away. As he looked out across the wintry hills, he saw fields of ripe blueberries and saw himself racing through the low bushes with his friends, trying to be the first to fill his shiny tin pail. He saw Mrs. Olson's house in Cushing, Maine, and saw her sitting in her wheelchair on the front porch, staring out at the blue sea. Then he looked closer to home and saw Karl Kuerner's old white farmhouse with the railroad tracks stretching past it. It was on those tracks that Jamie's grandfather had been killed. Jamie remembered the rusty metal sign: RAILROAD CROSSING—STOP, LOOK, AND LISTEN, and he thought of his grandfather's old car, stalled on the tracks, and the freight train racing down upon it.

In his mind Jamie was at home, fishing in the Brandywine River. He was playing by the old grain mill that his mother was busily working to restore. He was the hero in one of his grandfather's illustrations. He was Robin Hood leading the men of the greenwood through Sherwood Forest, and Captain Billy Bones in *Treasure Island*, keeping watch with his large brass telescope.

Jamie rose slowly. He felt the chill of the damp ground beginning to reach deep inside him. It was time to head home. He walked slowly across the fields and into the old farmhouse. He found his mother reading by the fire.

46

"Hello, Jamie," she said, looking up. "Where have you been?"

"Oh, everyplace, I guess," replied Jamie, and he was telling the truth. For in his mind Jamie had been Faraway.

CLEOBUS AND BITON
page 6

"Cleobus" and "Biton" are examples of Archaic Greek sculpture. The statues, called "kouroi" because *kouros* means "boy" in Greek, are some of the earliest representations of the human body in Greek art. The typical kouros stands stiffly with his left leg in front of his right. The details of his body, his face, and his hair are stylized into very unlifelike patterns. This is common to all Archaic art. The statues are signed by a sculptor from Argos named Polymedes. Their great size and well-crafted, sturdy forms reflect the power and artistic prominence of Argos in the early part of the sixth century before Christ.

DONATELLO (1386–1466)
page 9

Donatello was born in Florence, Italy. As a boy, he was apprenticed to a famous sculptor named Ghiberti. He also studied under a goldsmith, learned the art of engraving, and was a painter, an engineer, and an architect. The marble statue of David is six feet three inches high. At his feet is the head of Goliath, and on Goliath's forehead is a rock. Donatello sculpted David and Goliath four times, twice in marble and twice in bronze. For him, David was the perfect symbol of freedom and of youthful courage. The wreath of amaranth flowers on his head symbolizes the everlasting fame of the brave.

JAN VAN EYCK (?–1441)
page 10

It is not known exactly when or where in the Netherlands Jan Van Eyck was born. In 1422 he began to work as an artist for John of Bavaria, count of Holland. In 1425 he was appointed court painter to Duke Philip the Good of Burgundy. The duke sent Van Eyck all over Europe to paint portraits of ladies he was considering marrying. In 1429 Van Eyck was in Portugal at the court of King John I, painting Princess Isabella, whom the duke was to marry. In 1430 Van Eyck moved to Bruges, where he died in 1441. It is thought that Jan Van Eyck was trained by his older brother, Hubert, with whom he painted the Ghent Altarpiece.

PIETER BRUEGHEL (1527–69)
page 13

Pieter Brueghel was born somewhere near the border of Belgium and Holland. As a young boy he was apprenticed to a local painter. In 1551 he entered the Antwerp Guild of Painters and then went on a long journey through France and Italy to study Italian painting and learn the art of engraving. In 1563 Brueghel moved to Brussels, Belgium, and married the daughter of his teacher. Brueghel was a clever, good-humored man who loved practical jokes. This is evident in his work. His painting "Children's Games," like most of Brueghel's work, shows the tiny details of daily life, of people at play or work. Brueghel loved painting the common peasant, and he was nicknamed "Peasant Brueghel." When he died in 1569 he left his wife and two young sons, Pieter the Younger and Jan the Elder. Both boys became famous painters themselves.

DIEGO RODRÍGUEZ de SILVA y VELÁZQUEZ (1599–1660)
page 15

Diego Rodríquez de Silva y Velázquez was born in Seville, Spain. At twelve he was apprenticed to Francisco Pacheco, and when he was eighteen he married the painter's daughter, Juana. When he was twenty-one Velázquez went to Madrid to visit the Royal Palace, and when he was only twenty-four he painted his first portrait of Spain's new king, Philip IV. The king took a great liking to Velázquez and appointed him the court painter. The princess, Infanta Margarita Teresa, was four years old when this portrait, "Las Meninas," was made. Velázquez became a great friend and confidant of the king and eventually he lived with the royal family. In 1659 Velázquez was made a knight by the Council of the Order of Santiago.

THE LIMNER
page 17

Although the name of this artist is not known, a painting such as this is referred to as a limner painting. A limner was a portrait painter. The limner traveled all over New England in the 1600s and 1700s, painting portraits of families. Often he was an artist without formal art training. The artists were thought of only as craftsmen. This is the reason they rarely signed their works. The limner painted many families in one town. If people liked his portraits, he might spend an entire winter in the town, painting, and then move on in the spring.

SIR JOSHUA REYNOLDS
(1723–92)
page 18

Sir Joshua Reynolds was one of the greatest English portrait painters. He was the first president of the Royal Academy of the Arts. In 1784 he was made painter to the king of England, George III. Sir Joshua was also a writer. He helped to found the Literary Club, along with the famous British author Dr. Samuel Johnson. Reynolds was born in Plympton Earl, in Devonshire, England. He lived most of his life in London, and it was there he painted many of his famous portraits.

JOSEPH BADGER (1708–65)
page 21

Joseph Badger was born in Charlestown, Massachusetts. He lived in the Boston area until his death in 1765. Before becoming a portrait painter, Badger was a sign and house painter and a glazier (one who puts glass into windows). He had no formal art training, but he learned to paint from looking at prints and other art-ists' paintings. He is thought to have been the first American to specialize in realistic likeness. Approximately eighty portraits were painted by Badger in the last twenty-two years of his life, and many of these he did not sign.

FRANCISCO JOSÉ de GOYA y LUCIENTES (1746–1828)
page 22

Francisco José de Goya y Lucientes was born in the small village of Fuendetodos in Spain. Although his parents were very poor, they encouraged his painting. At seventeen he went to Madrid, the capital of Spain, to practice his art. At twenty-three he traveled to Italy and became inspired by the masterpieces of Italian art. After returning to Spain, he began painting frescoes—paintings of wet plaster—for chapels and churches. Goya was then hired by the Royal Tapestry Manufactory as a designer to produce "cartoons" for tapestries. He also became famous as a portrait painter. In 1788 he was commissioned by the Count of Altamira to paint the count's son, Don Manuel Osorio. In 1789 Goya was appointed "painter to the royal chamber," and in 1799 he became "first painter to the king," Charles IV.

EDWARD HICKS (1780–1849)
page 24

Edward Hicks, born in Newtown, Pennsylvania, was a carriage decorator and a sign painter. He was also a very faithful Quaker. Hicks considered his religion first, and he traveled all around the eastern United States preaching the word of the Bible. Many of his paintings depict scenes from the Bible. Hicks did not receive any formal training in his art. Because his forms do not appear lifelike, his animals don't look real, and his children look like miniature adults, Hicks has been called a "primitive painter." "The Peaceable Kingdom" is a famous piece of American primitive art.

EDOUARD MANET (1832–83)
page 26

Edouard Manet was born in Paris, France. He always wanted to be an artist, but his father thought he should study law. Because they could not agree on a profession, he and his father compromised on a naval career. After Edouard failed his naval

examinations twice, his father finally allowed him to study painting. From the beginning, very few people liked his paintings. They thought he painted ugly and vulgar pictures. But because some people liked his work and because he was happy painting, he continued to paint. It was not until he died that he became famous for those paintings that many people once considered ugly.

JAMES ABBOTT McNEILL WHISTLER (1834–1903)
page 28

James Abbott McNeill Whistler was born in Lowell, Massachusetts. Although he was an American painter, he lived in Europe most of his life. He was a realist painter—one who paints objects to look as if they are real. Whistler was considered a master colorist. Because of his love for color and music, he borrowed names from the field of music to describe his paintings, calling them "nocturnes," "arrangements," "symphonies," and "harmonies." Today the naming of paintings with musical names is accepted, but during Whistler's lifetime he was laughed at and criticized. Now his paintings are hung in museums and he is a well-known artist. He died in Europe.

WINSLOW HOMER (1836–1910)
page 30

Winslow Homer was born in Boston, Massachusetts. He started his art career as an illustrator for a weekly magazine. Then Homer decided he wanted to paint with watercolors and oils. He loved to paint scenes of children playing in the country, but later in his life he became famous for painting the sea and fishermen. Homer is best known for his watercolors. He lived much of his later years in Maine, and died there in 1910.

PIERRE-AUGUSTE RENOIR (1841–1919)
page 32

Pierre-Auguste Renoir began work at thirteen in Paris, where he painted porcelain in a factory. He began his career as an artist at twenty-one. Renoir was best known for his paintings of people—mainly women and children. He was one of the founders of the school of Impressionism—the style of art that is an immediate impression of the object. The artist painting in impressionistic style tries to show what the eye sees at a glance. Renoir was also famous for his sculpture. His wife, Aline, and his sons, Pierre, Claude, and Jean, were often his models.

MARY STEVENSON CASSATT (1845–1926)
page 35

Mary Stevenson Cassatt was an American impressionist. She studied at the Pennsylvania Academy of Fine Arts. She then went to Italy to study painting, and finally to Paris where she lived. She and Degas were very good friends. He helped her with her painting, and he was the teacher she admired most. Mary Cassatt's paintings were not readily accepted while she was alive. It was not thought fitting that a young woman should go to another country and try to enter a man's profession. Now her paintings belong to great museums and are admired all over the world.

EDGAR DEGAS (1834–1917)
page 36

Edgar Degas was born in Paris, France. His father was a wealthy French banker, and his mother was an American from New Orleans. Although Degas's father hoped Edgar would study law and go into the banking business, Edgar was interested only in drawing. Finally the family agreed to let him study art. His work centered almost exclusively on three subjects—the ballet, the theater, and the race course. Degas was fascinated by movement and by the human body. The "Dancer at the Age of Fourteen" is a bronze cast from a wax sculpture which Degas exhibited in Paris in 1881. The public was confused and embarrassed by the work, and called it ugly and "disagreeable." One critic reported hearing fathers exclaim, "Heaven grant that my daughter never becomes a dancer!"

JOHN SINGER SARGENT (1856–1925)
page 39
John Singer Sargent was an American citizen but he did most of his painting in England. Although he is best known as a portrait painter, his murals in the Boston (Massachusetts) Public Library are highly praised. They took twenty-seven years to complete. "Carnation, Lily, Lily, Rose" was painted in the Cotswold district of England. Sargent used the two daughters of an English friend as models. The painting continued into the winter months, and Sargent bought the girls long white woolen underwear to wear under their dresses so they would not get too cold while posing. He also purchased fresh flowers daily for the several months it took him to complete the painting. He died in London.

HENRI ROUSSEAU (1844–1910)
page 41
Henri Rousseau was born in Laval, France. His family was very poor and discouraged him from studying painting, hoping he could earn more money in the military service. After a brief military career, he returned to Laval and became a toll collector at the customs house. He is sometimes called "Le Douanier," the customs officer. At forty-nine Rousseau quit work to devote his life to painting. He was the object of ridicule and scorn. Critics poked fun at his work, saying it looked like the work of a child. But Rousseau kept painting, carefully showing all the tiny details in the patterns of nature. Rousseau is famous for his use of bright color and depiction of exotic, junglelike material. Some call him

"the master of trees." Though he was very poor throughout his life, Rousseau is now recognized as one of France's greatest artists. The painting "Baby's Party" was also called "Child with Punch." He painted this on commission and worked hard and for a long time on all the minute details.

GEORGE LUKS (1867–1933)
page 42
George Luks was an American painter. He was born in Williamsport, Pennsylvania. Luks started his career as a newspaper artist for the Philadelphia *Press*. After studying in Germany and France, he went to New York and worked as a cartoonist for the New York *World*. Then he turned to painting city life. He was interested in showing children playing in the streets, factory workers, and the slums. Luks was also a boxer, and he painted many pictures of fighters. Luks wanted other American artists to paint happenings in their own cities, but he wasn't able to persuade many to follow his ideas.

HENRY MOORE (1898–   )
page 45
Henry Moore was born in Castleford, Yorkshire, England. After brief service in World War I, he returned home to study at the Leeds School of Art. In 1921 he won a scholarship in sculpture and entered the Royal College of Art. Three years later he became an instructor there. In 1929 Moore was married to Irina Radetzky, and in 1946 his daughter Mary was born. In addition of thousands of small works like the "Rocking Chair," Moore has produced many huge outdoor sculptures which are exhibited all over Europe and the United States. He deals primarily with two main motifs—the mother and child, and the reclining figure. Moore has received worldwide recognition.

ANDREW WYETH (1917–   )
page 46
Andrew Wyeth is the son of the well-known illustrator N. C. Wyeth. He grew up in Chadds Ford, Pennsyl-

vania, and paints many scenes both of that area and of the area around his home in Cushing, Maine. "Faraway" is a painting of his son, Jamie. The technique is called "dry-brush watercolor": the artist draws with a very fine watercolor brush and then paints with watercolors to complete the picture. Jamie is now grown and a famous artist himself.

ACKNOWLEDGMENTS

Permission to reproduce the works of art in this book has been granted by:

Cleobus and *Biton*, Polymedes. Alison Frantz.

David, Donatello. Alinari-Art Reference Bureau.

Madonna and Chancellor Rolin, Jan Van Eyck. Alinari-Art Reference Bureau.

Children's Games, Pieter Brueghel the Elder. Kunsthistorischen Museum, Vienna, Austria.

Las Meninas, Diego Rodríquez de Silva y Velázquez. Anderson-Art Reference Bureau.

The Mason Children, Artist Unknown. Anonymous Collection.

Master Crewe as Henry III, Sir Joshua Reynolds. Collection of the Lord O'Neill.

Henry VIII, Hans Holbein the Younger. The Walker Art Gallery, Liverpool.

Portrait of Two Children, Joseph Badger. Abby Aldrich Rockefeller Folk Art Collection, Williamsburg, Virginia.

Don Manuel Osorio de Zuñiga, Francisco José de Goya y Lucientes. The Metropolitan Museum of Art, The Jules S. Bache Collection, 1949.

The Peaceable Kingdom, Edward Hicks. Worcester Art Museum, Worcester, Massachusetts.

The Fifer, Edouard Manet. Louvre, Jeu de Paume, National Museums, Paris.

Harmony in Gray and Green: Portrait of Miss Cicely Alexander, James Abbott McNeill Whistler. The Tate Gallery, London.

The Watermelon Boys, Winslow Homer. Courtesy of Cooper-Hewitt Museum, The Smithsonian Institution's National Museum of Design.

Madame Charpentier and Her Children, Pierre-Auguste Renoir. The Metropolitan Museum of Art, Wolfe Fund, 1907.

Woman and Child Driving, Mary Stevenson Cassatt. Philadelphia Museum of Art: Purchased: The W. P. Wilstach Collection.

A Dancer at the Age of Fourteen, Edgar Degas. The Metropolitan Museum of Art, Bequest of Mrs. H. O. Havemeyer, 1929, The H. O. Havemeyer Collection.

Carnation, Lily, Lily, Rose, John Singer Sargent. The Tate Gallery, London.

Baby's Party, Henri Rousseau. Kunstverein Winterthur, Winterthur, Switzerland.

The Spielers, George Luks. Addison Gallery of American Art, Phillips Academy.

Rocking Chair #3, Henry Moore. Collection of the Artist.

Faraway, Andrew Wyeth. Private Collection.